I CHOOSE
to Be Thankful

I CHOOSE SERIES

ELIZABETH ESTRADA

Copyright 2022 by Elizabeth Estrada - All rights reserved.
Published and printed in the USA.

No part of this publication or the information in it may be quoted or reproduced in any form by means of printing, scanning, photocopying, or otherwise without permission of the copyright holder.

I CHOOSE
to Be Thankful

ELIZABETH ESTRADA

I look around me
At all that I have.
I choose to be thankful,
Grateful and glad!

I choose to be thankful for my toys,
Of which I have so many.
Any time I want a new toy,
I remember I have plenty!

I choose to be thankful for my room,
It's my very own space.
This is the part of my home
That is my very favorite place.

I choose to be thankful for my mom.
She cares for me every day.
And showers me with love
In so many thoughtful ways.

She cooks for me,
And listens to me all the time.
I'm thankful for a mother,
As wonderful as mine!

I choose to be thankful for my dad
Who teaches me so much.
He reads to me and plays with me,
And even packs my lunch.

My father plays ball with me,
Out back in the yard.
Because of his encouragement,
I've learned to kick it far.

I choose to be thankful for my grandparents
Who always give me treats.
My grandma bakes me apple pie,
And plenty of other sweets!

The time we spend together
Is very special to me.
There's no place like my grandparents' house
That I would rather be.

I choose to be thankful for my teachers
Who are patient with me as I learn.
They help me understand my lessons,
So that good grades can be earned.

From math problems to reading,
They make time at school fun.
I don't even want to leave
When the school day is done.

I choose to be thankful for my bus driver
Who cares about my safety.
He drives the bus with care,
And is always polite and friendly.

I choose to be thankful for my doctor
Who is kind during my checkup.
She makes sure all is well,
As I grow and develop.

I choose to be thankful for my friends
Who listen and support me.
They accept me for who I am,
And like me because I'm me!

We celebrate each other's birthdays
Throughout the years.
They help me overcome obstacles
And help me face my fears.

I choose to be thankful for my pets.
They are gentle and sweet.
They're always sitting by me,
Or curling up at my feet.

I choose to be thankful
For all the wonderful people around me.
I am so grateful and happy
To have my friends and family.

I choose to be thankful
For all that surrounds me,
Because being a thankful person
Is a fantastic thing to be!